THE

FACTOR

A 30 DAY DEVOTIONAL

FAYE SHAW

THE *Favor* FACTOR

A 30 DAY DEVOTIONAL

FAYE SHAW

T&J PUBLISHERS

A SMALL INDEPENDENT PUBLISHER WITH A BIG VOICE

Printed in the United States of America by
T&J Publishers (Atlanta, GA.)
www.TandJPublishers.com

Cover Design by The epiMediaGroup, LLC (www.epimediagroup.com)

Book Format/Layout by Timothy Flemming, Jr. (T&J Publishers)

ISBN: 978-1-7335470-4-8

To contact author, go to:
www.IAmFayeShaw.com
Facebook: iamfayeshaw
Instagram: @_iamfayeshaw

For more information, contact:
PRTeam@epimediagroup.com

DEDICATIONS

Here are some well-deserved pats on some very strong backs:

Havell and Lavada Johnson - my parents, the real MVPs who introduced me to Christ. I will forever be indebted to you even as you are resting with the Savior. Thank you seems so inadequate.

Darrell Shaw - my husband, encourager, and my biggest support in ministry. Thank you, babe, for your patience in allowing God to use me for His purpose. Love you forever and then after that.

Kristen and Alexis - the best daughters a mother could ever ask for. Thanks for always encouraging me to reach higher and stretch for more.

Jalyn and Emerie - granddaughters that keep me on my toes! Just thank you for being authentically YOU!

Toya O'Neal, Darlene Foote, Brittany Nelson - project manager and editors; thank you so much for keeping me on task and assisting me with this project. You're appreciated more than you'll ever know!

To my Johnson Family - thank you for ALWAYS showing me how much you love and care for me. Most of all, I thank God for the praying family members He's blessed me with. Love you all.

To my entire GCCC Family - I'm forever grateful to God for each one that God has allowed our paths to cross. Doing life and ministry together with you has been amazing! My Grace Rocks!

To YOU - the reader. May the real Author speak directly to you each day as you embark on this journey.

And most of all, to You, God. The only way we can experience favor is through You. So, before we even ask You for anything, we stop to say, THANK YOU Lord for all You've done for us!

Table of Contents

Foreword ix

Intro: Let's Do It Again... There's More In Store ... 11

Day 1: You Were Created For This ... 17

Day 2: Can You Hear Me Now? ... 21

Day 3: Whose Plan Are You Following? ... 25

Day 4: Faith Requires Action ... 29

Day 5: Stay On The Wall ... 33

Day 6: Celebrate The Mile Markers ... 37

Day 7: Dispel Doubt During Delay ... 41

Day 8: Slow Down And Enjoy The Journey ... 45

Day 9: Leave It There ... 49

Day 10: Don't Miss Your Miracle ... 53

Day 11: Don't Despise The Detour ... 55

Day 12: When The Odds Are Against You ... 57

Day 13: No Unmet Needs ... 61

Day 14: Don't Just Talk About It ... 65

Day 15: He's More Than A Feeling ... 69

Day 16: He's All You Need ... 73

Day 17: Count Your Blessings ... 77

Day 18: The Door Is Open, Your Move ... 81

Day 19: Know Your Assignment ... 85

Day 20: It's Time To Focus On The "But" ... 89

Day 21: He Can Use You Anyway   93

Day 22: Living My Best Life   97

Day 23: Someone Is Assigned To You   101

Day 24: Keeping Up With Christ   105

Day 25: A Greater Call   109

Day 26: The Power Of A Closed Mouth   113

Day 27: Your Name Is Servant   117

Day 28: Simply Trust   121

Day 29: Love Them Anyway   125

Day 30: The Glory From Your Story   129

Outro: Congratulations!   133

Foreword

IT IS AN HONOR AND A PRIVILEGE TO WRITE THIS FOREWORD AND to share with you about my friend and sister in ministry, Wanda Faye Shaw. She is truly a Proverbs 31 Woman.

I have known her and her family, for more than 40 years. Her parents, siblings, husband, children, and grandchildren have shown their faith in the Lord by their faithful witness and lifestyle.

Now, she shares the secret to her success, and that of her family - The Favor Factor. She and her family have accomplished so much by the grace of God.

Faye, as we affectionately call her, opens her heart and exudes with exuberance the excitement of experiencing the favor of God and how it will revolutionize your life.

In this 30- day devotional, Faye will walk you step by step to a closer relationship with the Almighty God and how He will bring about significant, positive change in your life. She will show you how, with His favor, you can truly live your best life.

Experience it now, The Favor Factor! The best is yet to come!

John E. King, Jr.
Pastor, Trinity Baptist Church
Birmingham, Alabama

Let's Do It Again... There's More In Store

N THE ORIGINAL VERSION OF *THE FAVOR FACTOR*, THERE were daily devotionals to help you recognize God's favor and the impact it has on your life, but there is something more that I need to share in this edition. Warning … it will require a little more work and effort on your part, but I promise that it will be well worth it. There have been times, when I have been blessed by simply listening to God's word, however when I become an active participant, whether voluntarily or involuntarily, that Word becomes seared in my heart and I gain so much more. So I'm here to ask are you, "Are you ready to get the more that God has for you?" Whether this is your first read of The Favor Factor, or you're doing it again, I believe that you will be even more encouraged to continue to trust that, not only does your Father, who favors you, hear you when you pray but will also see you in your situation because The Favor Factor is at work in your life.

I've been through many challenges to say the least, since I penned the original version. I've experienced first-hand how God can take the most tumultuous storms and cause "Peace be Still" moments that can only be explained as the grace of God. In other words, FAVOR. I've added this chapter to encourage you to realize that when God places favor on your life, it's designed to last a lifetime. It's written in the Word of God. It's found in the book of Psalm 30:5. What I love about favor is that it's not just for preachers, and I am one! It is, however, for the righteous. Uh oh. Watch this; not perfect, but righteous. Now, you may be saying, "where did she get that from?" Well, Psalm 5:12 says, "Surely, Lord, you bless the righteous; you surround them with your favor as with a shield." What does it mean to be righteous? The dictionary defines righteous as: one of good character, integrity, good moral behavior, (even when no one is looking), virtue. So, you see, you don't have to be perfect. We all make mistakes. And guess what? God absolutely knew we would make mistakes before He created us, and He still loves us! So, repent of your sins, get back on track, and experience this favor I'm talking about if you're not already there.

As I was saying, life was going very well, and things were looking great and then.... something changed. Some things changed. Some situations changed. Life as I knew it, changed. During this time, I felt like I was on a roller coaster and needed to get off because I was experiencing the effects of "spiritual vertigo." Vertigo is a

Intro

sensation of feeling off balance. It's like your very foundation, the place that's always secure, is literally moving under your feet. As a result, you experience dizzy spells, sometimes it feels like you are spinning and other times it feels like the world around you is spinning. That's what happened to me. It was like, one day everything in my life was in order and suddenly, chaos began to wreak havoc from every direction imaginable. I was knocked down by life's challenges. They were coming faster than I thought I could recover.

As soon as I would get up, another storm would hit. Just like the side effects of vertigo, as I would get up, I would become dizzy and lightheaded at the thought of trying to get my balance after the last experience. This would happen repeatedly. I began to wonder, what in the world was going on. I even found myself upset with God because I knew that I was trying to live a holy and righteous life. Have you been there? If so, I encourage you to keep reading because I promise you it's going to get better! You see, I understood I would have trials and tribulations but.... when was it going to end? I was really growing weary.

The Favor Factor

I can now say that I know how David must have felt when he said in Psalm 27:13 (TLB) "I am expecting the Lord to rescue me again, so that once again I will see his goodness to me here in the land of the living." Despite David's circumstances, how he felt or what he saw, he expected God to come through! Now, let's get ready for the SHIFT! The Favor Factor! God showed me this scripture in this version because of the word, again. Again, means another time, once more. As I said at the beginning of this chapter, God is the God of "come through." He WILL rescue. Just when I thought I couldn't make it through another storm, God reminded me of not only who I am, but Who He is! Yes, I'm more than a conqueror, but it is God who has fought my battles. My assignment during that season was to stand still. When my flesh wanted to give out, give up, walk away, and throw in the towel, it is God who kept me and that's FAVOR. It's the supernatural power of the almighty God who had His hands on me and He put a smile on my face and peace in my spirit that was inexplicable.

There were those that knew of the various challenges that I was facing, and they were very concerned. They would ask me if I was okay, and I'm sure some of them thought I was having some sort of breakdown. But, I would just smile and say, "I'm good." I'm sure they were wondering, "How can she say she's good?" You know how I could say I was good? Because I thoroughly examined Psalm 27:13 (TLB) and David begins with "I am expecting the Lord to rescue me." Come through God! Favor will show up! I'm a living witness that it will! The key component is living in expectation. Favor is a lifestyle for a lifetime. That's why David can say that he's expecting the Lord to come through again. God doesn't bless us like an item at the department store semi-annual sale. David can probably say again because he had already experienced the Lord as being his shepherd in Psalm 23 where he finds Him as comforter, keeper, and One who restores his soul.

Intro

Watch this: When you walk (live) in expectation that the God we serve will rescue (come through), AGAIN, you WILL SEE HIS GOODNESS HERE in the land of the living! Yes, going to heaven is going to be great, but don't discount the experience of the abundant life you have right here on earth! Please know that homes, cars, clothes, shoes, trips, etc. are great and I love them all, but may I please share some more abundant living with you? Salvation, unspeakable joy, renewed strength, peace of mind, ability to walk, talk, have eyes AND can see ... these are priceless.

You were created with favor in mind and God has His eyes on you. I don't know where you are in life right now, but I do know that no matter where you are, God can set you in a place of favor in such a way that even your enemies won't be able to deny the hand of God is on your life.

Faith in Action

Even if you read the original version of The Favor Factor, I encourage you to read it again and again ... there is no such thing as too much Favor from God. I believe God will give you fresh revelations. However, this time you have to be an active participant. Each devotion will end with a Daily Declaration that will serve to seal truths about God's Favor and enable you to declare God's principles over your life each day. Additionally, there is a Favor Factor Companion Journal that will enable you to delve deeper into the lesson and record what it means to you and how it impacts your life. As you read about God's favor you will come to realize that when

The Favor Factor

God places favor on your life, it's designed to last a life-time.

Daily Declaration

Today, I'm a winner. No matter what it looks like, I can't lose. My God will come through AGAIN and AGAIN and AGAIN. The Favor Factor is at work in my life!

You Were Created For This

"I praise you because I am fearfully and wonderfully made; your works are wonderful, I know that full well." – Psalm 139:14

ISN'T IT SIMPLY AMAZING TO KNOW THAT GOD TOOK THE time to create you in such a way that there is absolutely no one like you? Others may tell you that you look like your mother or act just like your father, but the fact of the matter is you are an original!

God took the time to shape and mold you just the way you are. We spend so much time and money (that we really don't have) trying to change what God created. We attempt to adapt to what society deems as beautiful. God gives us black hair, we want blonde! God gives us brown eyes and we want green. He created us to be a size 14, but we want to be a size 6!

The Favor Factor

Understand that God is into customization! He customized you for a particular purpose. He made you not because He didn't have anything else to do, but because He intended for you to worship Him. Once we understand that we are fearfully and wonderfully made, we can focus on the reason we were created. We must recognize that God made us and appreciate the details that went into our design. God even knows the number of hairs on our heads (including weave)! Isn't that amazing? He loves us that much.

What we must also understand is that even though we know that God loves us, there are going to be challenges that we must face in this life. These challenges will sometimes cause us to say, "why me?" The real question, however, becomes, "why not you?" Understand that whatever storm you may be facing right now; you were created for it! The same way that God took the time to create you, He also put something on the inside of you to equip you with the ability to handle what He gives you.

Today we will focus on the fact that God created us to worship Him and minister on His behalf. This means that as His children, storms are part of our assignment. Because we are favored, God has already spoken our victory over the storm so that others can see Him working in our lives.

The Favor Factor

Storms are a part of life. You may be wondering, "Where is The Favor Factor?" Well, here it is. The Favor Factor is that although you WILL (not may) face storms in your

Day 1

life, Jesus says that He will be there, right smack dab in the middle of it! Remember the raging storm at sea when the disciples were on the boat, and Jesus was right there with them? He was LITERALLY right there! Yes, as man, He was asleep, but don't you think for one minute that He was unaware of the storm. What I'm saying to you right now is that just because it appears that Jesus may be napping through your raging storm, please know that He's well aware of it, because you were created for it!

Faith in Action

You may be thinking, "I don't know how this is going to work out; but what I'm saying to you is that because you are favored, you already have the victory. Jesus is speaking directly to your storm saying, "Peace be still." Focus not on your situation; focus on your favor! Right now declare, "God brought me to this storm, and God will see me through this storm." Why? Because you were created for this!

Daily Declaration

I am a one-of-a-kind original. God designed me to face and conquer every challenge and storm that comes my way today. I am already victorious because of God's Favor on my life.

The Favor Factor

Can You Hear Me Now?

"Be still, and know that I am God: I will be exalted among the heathen, I will be exalted in the earth."
– Psalm 46:10

TOP COMPLAINING THAT GOD'S NOT SPEAKING, AND listen to what He's telling you. We ask God for things, and it often seems as though it's taking forever for Him to answer. We will say things like, "I've prayed about my situation, but God hasn't said anything, so I'm just going to have to wait." In some instances, this is very true, but there are times when we think God hasn't answered our prayers when in fact He has already answered them through people and through His Word.

Our connection with God during the good times is critical and alleviates the tendency to disconnect from

Him when confusion, rejection, or painful experiences occur.

The problem is not that God isn't speaking, but rather we have a problem with our hearing. Sometimes God is silent because He's already answered our questions. Think about a parent. If a child asks the parent a question and the parent has answered, the parent isn't going to continue to answer the same question over and over again. The same is true with our Father; we must learn to fine tune our hearing and understand that God is always speaking to us whether through a song, a message, a book, a person or His Word.

The Favor Factor

The Favor Factor is that we are privileged to be able to have a one-on-one conversation with God; and we can expect Him to answer. When I was growing up, we were taught not to question God. I've learned that although I may not have a right to question God, He does allow me to ask questions.

Faith in Action

Why not ask your questions to the One who can answer? Go ahead, ask Him now, stop talking and complaining, and listen to what He has to say.

Day 2

Daily Declaration

Today, I refuse to complain about anything. I will be still and know that you are God. As your favored, I know Your will is what's best for me. Today, I will hear and obey.

The Favor Factor

Whose Plan Are You Following?

"For I know the plans I have for you,' declares the Lord, 'plans to prosper you and not to harm you, plans to give you hope and a future." – Jeremiah 29:11

MANY TIMES WE BEGIN TO "MAKE" OUR OWN PLANS and then after our plans don't go as intended, we become frustrated, agitated, disgusted, and disappointed. We start questioning "why" things didn't work out after we spent so much time planning. Today we will discover that God has orchestrated a life that is unimaginable for those He favors. He had a plan designed for us before we were even born. That plan is far greater than any plan we could even conceive. The sooner we accept God's direction, the sooner we live the life that He intended for us.

The Favor Factor

One reason I've found that our plans don't work out is because we "make" plans without consulting the One who "knows" the plans! We plan everything from where we will go to college, who and when we will marry, how many kids we will have, where we will work, what kind of house we will buy, and what kind of car we will drive. The truth is that we really don't have to worry about any of those things. As one who knows that you are favored, you can rest in the assurance of what His Word says in Jeremiah 29:11.

God never says that we will know or even understand the plans. What He does say though, is that He "knows" the plans. This means that we don't have to "make" them because God already has everything under control. He is so into you and I that He even gives us a glimpse of the plans. He says His plans are to give us hope and a future. He also says that His plans are not designed to harm us but to prosper us. Isn't that wonderful?

In Jeremiah 1:4-5, God tells Jeremiah that before he was formed in his mother's womb, God knew him. God tells Jeremiah that He has set him apart. It sounds to me as though God already had a plan for Jeremiah even before he was born.

The Favor Factor

The Favor Factor is that God KNEW you BEFORE your mama met your daddy! In fact, He knew every valley and mountaintop experience you would have in your life. He knew that you would make wrong choices and bad decisions. He knew that you would go places that

Day 3

you shouldn't go, do the things that you shouldn't have done, and say the things you shouldn't have said.

You may be reading this right now and wondering how this can be favor. Let me tell you. Not only does God know you, He set you apart! Although you may not feel like you're where you should be in life right now, it's all part of the plan! God sees something in you that you cannot see in yourself. Sometimes it takes us longer to reach our destiny because we want God to join us after we've made plans, and He's simply not going to do that. For example, we ask God to bless our marriage at the wedding ceremony but don't once consult Him before we accept the ring. We say things like, "God please change my spouse," when in fact that's not even the person God planned for you to marry. But do you know what else is a Favor Factor? Despite all of the things we may have done wrong, there is this five letter word called "grace" that God gives us, and it allows us to bounce back from our man-made plans. It's unmerited favor! We can't work for it, and we can't pay for it! We don't deserve it; yet God extends it to us.

Faith in Action

So at this very moment, instead of asking God to help you with your plans, thank Him for His plans, and join Him now where He is at work in your life!

The Favor Factor

Daily Declaration

You have great plans for my life, plans to prosper, give me hope and a future. Therefore, I will
not fear what lies ahead. I refuse to detour --
your plans lead to my destiny.

Faith Requires Action

"In the same way, faith by itself, if it is not accompanied by action, is dead." – James 2:17

I t's time to put our faith in action! Faith is not waiting for God to perform. Faith is working toward the evidence of things not seen. Think about this; a person believes that he/she can lose weight and live a healthier lifestyle, but to accomplish those goals, that person must put in some work such as exercising and eating healthy. As those actions happen, manifestation takes place.

Today we will realize we recognize that faith without works is dead. This means that we cannot just say that we have faith in what God has spoken; we must work that faith (be unwavering; be obedient to His direction) in order to see it manifest.

We can call on God and confer with God, but we must come to a point of having the confidence that's needed to know beyond the shadow of any doubt that God is willing and able to do what He says He will do. My Pastor often says that faith is believing that a thing is so, even when it isn't so, in order that it may be so. Even when we can't see how it will happen, we must have faith that it will happen. However, we must also put in the action to make it happen. If we do our part, God will honor that and do His. He is a supernatural God so if we just handle our end, God will add the "super" to our natural to create the manifestation of what we are believing for. We have to work with our faith in order to see our faith work in our favor.

The Favor Factor

The Favor Factor comes in knowing that we have direct access to God. We don't have to go through anyone to talk to Him. We have that one-on-one connection to receive clear instruction, understand His vision, and learn exactly what He wants us to do. We don't have to hear it from anyone else and risk our direction getting lost in translation. Because we are able to get direction straight from the source, we must have confidence that what He has spoken will come to pass. No matter how uncomfortable or even strange our directions may be, we must have confidence that if God said it, it will work. There is another Favor Factor here; we are so favored that whenever we "mess up" or become unclear about what God said, we can always go back for redirection.

Day 4

God is always ready to guide us, and He doesn't just hear us, but He answers every time we call. Truth be told, we may not always like or want to hear the answer He gives, but we must have faith in knowing that whatever He promises, He will bring it to pass.

Faith in Action

Work your faith and watch God perform His perfect will in your life.

Daily Declaration

Today I put my faith into action. Now faith is the substance of things hoped for, the evidence of things not seen. I will work my faith in order to see faith work in my favor.

The Favor Factor

Stay On The Wall

"Therefore, my dear brothers and sisters, stand firm. Let nothing move you. Always give yourselves fully to the work of the Lord, because you know that your labor in the Lord is not in vain." – 1 Corinthians 15:58

OFTENTIMES, WE ARE GIVEN ASSIGNMENTS IN LIFE and if we aren't careful, we will allow Satan to distract us from keeping the main thing the main thing. During the journey of life, we will have obstacles and roadblocks along the way, but we must remain focused on the destination. Stay on the wall!

Today we learn how to remain focused on God. When on the ladder, it's imperative to find a focal point. We can't look down at what is going on below because it causes imbalance and the potential for a fall. Keep focused on the task and complete the assignment. God's favor provides strength when we feel like giving up.

When Nehemiah was rebuilding the wall in Nehemiah Chapter 6, there were some naysayers at the bottom of the ladder who were asking him to come down and meet with them. He refuses to come down. What he was really saying was that he didn't have time to waste. There was no time to talk to people whose mouths were moving but weren't really saying anything! How many times have we allowed detractors and distractions to knock us so far off course that we lose the drive to continue our journey? By recognizing beforehand those people and things that have the potential to knock us off the wall, we can avoid those pitfalls before they happen.

Remember that nothing about our situation surprises God. He allows distractions to test us and rewards us for passing the test. Our naysayers and enemies are actually an important part of getting through our journey. They were designed to help strengthen our focus on God, our destination, and our will. Keeping the focus on God and off of distractions shows God just how serious we are and even accelerates us to reach our goal.

The Favor Factor

Don't become distracted by your obstacles, it will only slow you down. It can also cause an imbalance and throw you off track. Things that should take one week will end up taking one month because we've been sidetracked. Stay focused and don't allow anyone to get you off the ladder until your assignment is complete. Even when it gets rough, and it will, God will give you the favor that's needed to finish what He started in you! The Favor Factor in all of this is that whenever we feel weak, God is right there to strengthen us. He will even take on our challenges when they become too much to handle. Understand that with God, you have every single thing that you need to stay on the wall!

Faith in Action

Take a moment now and identify the distractions that have caused you to lose focus. Determine that you will not let these slow you down, recommit to your assignment and get back on the wall.

Daily Declaration

Today, I refuse to be distracted, discouraged or disturbed by obstacles that come my way. I will remain steadfastly focused on the mission God has put before me. Today, The Favor Factor is at work in my life.

The Favor Factor

Celebrate The Mile Markers

"And we know that in all things God works for the good of those who love him, who have been called according to his purpose." – Romans 8:28

THERE ARE SOME DECISIONS THAT WE MAKE IN LIFE that make us say, "If I had the chance to do it again, I would do some things differently." We must realize, though, that every detail of our lives, including those we deem as mistakes have already been taken into account by God. Remember that bad relationship? God already knew that would happen. He also knew that you would rebel against those who were trying to keep you from experiencing heartache. What we must remember is that those "mistakes" are part of the preparation! Once we come through bad experiences, we are ready for what God truly had waiting the

The Favor Factor

whole time!

Today we will focus on recognizing favor in situations that may look like mistakes or wasted time. But, God doesn't make mistakes; understand that everything that happens will work in your favor so that God can get the glory.

I made some unwise decisions early in life. But despite what I thought was trauma and tragedy, God's favor has allowed me to now experience tremendous overflow! That "unwise decision" was not a waste of my time. It was a part of the plan. Through it all, I learned what relationships are and aren't supposed to look like! What I want you to understand is even if you are not exactly where you think you should be at this very moment, favor is coming.

The Favor Factor

The Favor Factor comes as we see how God can take our mistakes and mess and turn it into miracles and ministry! You may have been beating yourself up over some things you should have done differently, but please know that God's hand is still on you and you are coming out! In the meantime, recognize that you are just working on your testimony! When God brings you out, you're going to be stronger and wiser. Can I tell you something else? A lot of what you're dealing with isn't even about you! Your testimony will serve as a witness to the world that if God can bring you out, He will bring them out as well! At the end of the day, The Favor Factor is that you won't look like what you've been through!

Day 6

Faith in Action

Declare right now that Today is working on my testimony day!

Daily Declaration

Whatever happens today, good, bad, ugly or in between, I will not worry or fear because I know that ALL things are working together for my good.

The Favor Factor

Dispel Doubt During Delay

"And we know that in all things God works for the good of those who love him, who have been called according to his purpose." – Romans 8:28

N TODAY'S SOCIETY, WE HAVE BECOME SO IMPATIENT. WE want everything instantaneously. Think about it. Instant grits, microwaveable food, drive-thru, one-hour cleaners, quick weight loss, high-speed internet, and same day dentures! The list goes on and on. During the journey of life, we can become discouraged because it seems like things are taking longer than we anticipated. However, if we aren't careful, we will allow doubt to creep into our mind during these times, and we will begin to question whether God will really come through.

Today focus on learning how to embrace the duration of your journey. Don't be moved by how long your breakthrough is taking to manifest. It's not that God doesn't have it for you; it's that YOU have not finished the preparation phase and are not quite ready to receive all that will come. He's shown you the land flowing with milk and honey, but are you ready to walk through your Red Sea to get there? Thank God for the basic training that He's taking you through to prepare you for the battles that will come along with your blessing.

God hasn't changed His mind nor has His ability to do what He promised changed. The question is, how bad do you really want it? Today's focal scripture talks about a land flowing with milk and honey. When we read this we get all excited about our overflow; but what happens when we find out we're going to have to go through a Red Sea? Sometimes there's a battle before the blessing.

Right now you may be thinking, I can see the light at the end of the tunnel, but, I'm still in the tunnel! Your Word for today is this: get rid of the doubt during the delay. God is going to do just what He said He would do. Yes, right now you may only see your enemy behind you and your Red Sea in front of you. Just hold on because you're getting ready to walk on dry land.

The Favor Factor

The Favor Factor is that you may be delayed but know you're not denied! You shall have what God says you will have! Please know that you're being set up for a supernatural shift to take place in your life! Hang on to what you know God told you no matter how it looks. God's

Word says that you are a lender and not a borrower. His Word says you are the head and not the tail. Believe it!

Faith in Action

Think about one thing that you gave up on because it was taking too long. Now determine and then declare that there will be no doubt during this delay.

Daily Declaration

Despite the delay, I will not doubt. God is going to do just what He said He would do. The Favor Factor is at work in my life!

The Favor Factor

Slow Down And Enjoy The Journey

"So I commend the enjoyment of life, because there is nothing better for a person under the sun than to eat and drink and be glad. Then joy will accompany them in their toil all the days of the life God has given them under the sun." – Ecclesiastes 8:15

SOMETIMES WE ARE IN SUCH A HURRY TO GET TO OUR destiny that we miss the journey along the way. God would not bless us with the trees, grass, sky, moon, stars, rain, ice, snow, seasons, and so many other wonderful things, if He didn't want us to enjoy them. Unfortunately, we spend so much energy on "getting" and "going" to our destination that we miss the beauty of the intricate details that God has laid out for us during the journey.

Today we focus on the beauty of the "scenery" of

The Favor Factor

life. Even though we may not have reached our desired destination, God continually blesses us along the way with tangible and intangible aspects that should not go unnoticed.

When I was in my early teens, I couldn't wait to become an adult. Oh, I was thinking about my apartment and my car only to find out it really wasn't nearly as great as I thought it would be. For some of us, our best years were our former years, but we didn't appreciate them because we were so focused on trying to become an adult. No bills, no mortgage, no responsibilities! We now realize there was no reason at all to rush into life. I thank God for His favor in that I can now look back and appreciate the full course meals we ate every day, how dinner was family time, and everyone was at the table together in the same room. That's called the scenery of life.

The Favor Factor

The Favor Factor comes from recognizing that God has placed treasures throughout the journey for us to enjoy on our way to destiny. Even if you're in a rough place right now, please know that it could be worse. God's favor is taking you to the place that He created just for you. Don't miss what He is saying to you along the way. You're going to get to your destination, but make sure you appreciate the journey along the way as my Uncle Bit says, "Make every day count."

Faith in Action

Take a moment to embrace and enjoy where you are

right now. Now take a deep breath and slow down, and take time to relax and appreciate where you are and the many treasures that surround you. Don't rush into where you're going but love where you are.

Daily Declaration

Today and every day is a gift. A day that I will never see again. So today, I will slow down, take in the day and all it has to offer, and embrace the journey. Every day is a good day for God's favored.

The Favor Factor

Leave It There

"Forget the former things; do not dwell on the past."
— Isaiah 43:18

T'S A BRAND NEW DAY! AREN'T YOU GLAD? ALTHOUGH LAST year, last month, last week, or even last night may have been a little rough, you made it! Are you ready to move into your new thing? There are a few things that I've learned in regards to moving. One thing is everything that is in your present isn't designed for your future. Secondly, you cannot move forward looking backward.

On this day understand that God is trying to move you closer to your destiny, but first you have to let go of those things and people who are not supposed to come with you.

The Favor Factor

There is a television program called Hoarders that shows how people accumulate things over the years, and as time moves on, they continue to store things and never move anything out. Their lives become a horrible mess but their living conditions are usually deplorable. A hoarder is described as one who feels the need to find, keep, collect, and pack any and everything because they do not know how to throw things away. Let's shift a little bit. We must not find, keep, collect, and pack our hurt, anger, disappointment, and unforgiving spirit because our lives will become a horrible mess, and the Spirit of God will not reside in an unclean place.

Isaiah 43:18 tells us to forget the former. Let's pause right there. God showed me a fresh revelation of how important it is to operate in those three words before we can even begin to experience the "new thing." He shared with me that it really doesn't matter what the former is. What do I mean? Your "former" may not have been bad at all. He doesn't say, "Forget the former bad stuff."

The Favor Factor

Here is The Favor Factor. God is saying to you and me that no matter how good or bad your life has been, and is right now, it gets better with the new thing! Everyone will have trials and tribulations, but it didn't say that everyone will experience tragedy and trauma.

As I said earlier, some things that are in your present aren't designed to go with you into your future. This includes people and places. The problem comes when we try to force a "past" or "former" thing to flow into the "new thing" category. We should be thankful for our past despite the challenges we may have faced. We've been taught to take back what the devil has stolen, but I'm encouraging you today to let him keep what he has taken because God is doing a new thing and what you're trying to hold on to or "take back" won't fit in your new place anyway.

Faith in Action

Stop looking back at what happened or didn't happen, what worked and didn't work. Looking back will only slow you down. Make a declaration today and say, "I'm forgetting the former and I'm flowing into my future because God is doing a new thing!" It's looking fabulous and it's called The Favor Factor!

Daily Declaration

No matter how good or bad life's been, better is on the way. Today, I press toward the mark of the prize of the high calling in Christ Jesus.

The Favor Factor

Don't Miss Your Miracle

"You are the God who performs miracles; you display your power among the peoples." — Psalm 77:14

TOO OFTEN WE FIND OURSELVES LOOKING FOR A miracle when in fact everything God does is a miracle. We say things like, "it's a miracle that I arrived to work on time because the traffic was so heavy." Although we don't think of it in that way, the reality is that yes, it is a miracle that you made it because someone didn't. God is telling us to stop looking for this big miracle to come our way and recognize that everything He does is big!

Today we will discover that God is always performing miracles, but we don't always notice it because we only recognize them in the form of what we want.

The Favor Factor

Opportunities are all around; don't miss them waiting on something that was never intended for you anyway.

The Favor Factor

The Favor Factor is realizing that it's a big deal to be able to breathe. It's a big deal to be able to see, walk, talk, smell, and think! That is a miracle! A miracle is God's extra on our ordinary; it's His super on our natural; it's His utter on our most! That's BIG! We serve a BIG God! You are a miracle! You don't have to wait for a miracle! Miracles occur every day all day. Don't miss them.

Faith in Action

Take a moment and thank God for all the miracles in your life, whether you consider them big or small.

Daily Declaration

I thank you for my breath, for the ability to stand and see the beauty of your Creation. Today I declare that you God are great, and so are each of Your miracles!

Don't Despise The Detour

"Then the Lord said to Moses, 'Tell the Israelites to turn back and encamp near Pi Hahiroth, between Migdol and the sea. They are to encamp by the sea, directly opposite Baal Zephon.'" – Exodus 14:1-2

SOME THINGS ARE DESIGNED TO TAKE US LONGER TO receive. Don't despise the detour of life. Sometimes we have to go the long way. The shortest route isn't always the best route, or the quickest route for that matter. Usually we don't like detours because they take us to unfamiliar territory. When traveling on a road we've never traveled, we must pay attention to the signs along the way in order to get to our destination. That's the way life goes sometimes as well.

Today we will learn that the shortest route is not always the best route. Sometimes, we must go the long way in life, it allows us to see the magnitude of God's love as He takes care of every detail along the way. That's His favor working on our behalf.

The Favor Factor

The Favor Factor here is knowing that God loves us so much that He will go out of His way to take us out of the way of trouble, tragedy, and trials. There are times when we will have to take the unfamiliar route. During those times we must depend on the signs that God shows us along the way. Sometimes He may tell us to stop, slow down, or switch lanes. Why? He has a vantage viewpoint that we don't. He knows where He's leading us, and He knows what lies ahead. God has a way of protecting us even when we don't want to be protected! He sees the harmful things that are in our path so He sometimes takes us through the detour. As tedious and frustrating as that can be, it is always worth it in the end.

Faith in Action

Go ahead and thank God for the detour. But more than that, thank Him for loving you enough to lead you through unknown dangers.

Daily Declaration

Today, I will follow wherever You lead. I will not fear the detour or unfamiliar for You are leading me through trouble, tragedy and trials I will never even see.

When The Odds Are Against You

"This is what the LORD says to you: 'Do not be afraid or discouraged because of this vast army. For the battle is not yours, but God's.'" – *2 Chronicles 20:15*

DURING THE JOURNEY OF LIFE, WE OFTEN END UP IN unintended places and situations. We make decisions that leave us asking ourselves, "What in the world was I thinking?" There are some "just this once" sins that we commit and, before we realize it, they have consumed us and kept us way longer than we planned. We end up doing things that we said we would never do; we go places that we said we would never go; and deal with people who normally would never get our attention.

Today, let's focus on God's odds-defying abilities.

The Favor Factor

No matter what life throws your way, you have to under-stand that nothing is too hard for God. Nothing catches Him by surprise, and nothing can stop Him from doing what He says He will do. What did He say? He said that we should not be afraid of how the situation looks like. When the odds are not in your favor, have peace and know that God will bring you out of whatever storm you face. He will fight our battles.

From all accounts, the idea of bouncing back and recovering from our mistakes look pretty grim (from our view anyway). If today's Favor Factor is speaking directly to you and where you are in your life right now, I have great news for you! God is in the odd-defying business! He absolutely LOVES to perform the supernatural. There are many stories in the Bible that show how God takes a situation that seems hopeless, steps in, and turns every-thing completely around. Think about the woman with the issue of blood. The odds were truly stacked against her. She had been dealing with her issue for 12 long years, and the Bible declares that she and her situation both grew worse. What do I mean? It says that she ex-hausted all of her resources. But despite the odds our Sovereign God, who loves to work against the odds, healed her body!

Can I share with you a little piece of my story? There's a little country girl from Birmingham, Alabama who grew up and became a little rebellious during her teenage years. Everything her family tried to tell her NOT to do, she DID! She made wrong choices and bad deci-sions that led to many consequences. Some of the deci-sions forced her into early adulthood. The likelihood of her succeeding in life as a professional and intelligent young woman looked very bleak. God had already pre-destined her for greatness though, and because He's unquestionably in charge of EVERYTHING, He took her and rearranged her life and turned what looked like a mess into ministry! God is into the odds-defying business!

Can I give you one more example? Look at how Jesus beat the odds! He had to carry His own weapon (the cross) that He knew would later kill Him; He endured the excruciating torture of being nailed to that cross by His hands and feet. He hung on that cross as others watched and mocked Him. He bled, suffered, and eventually died, all while knowing that He never did any wrong. He didn't just die though; He was also buried. Just when Satan thought that it was over, three days later Jesus got up from the grave with all power in His hands. What are the odds? It's called The Favor Factor, and you have that same power through God's favor.

The Favor Factor

Because of the Favor Factor, we can trust that God will defy the odds. You've come too far and cried too many tears to give up now. Are you a single parent or just lost your job? Maybe you are not doing well in school or you're physically sick. Whatever your situation may be, I'm here to encourage you and let you know that God is in the odds-defying business.

Faith in Action

This is your day! No matter how hard it's been or how

hard it is right now, please understand that God is going to turn your situation around. Keep trusting Him and have faith that it's all part of the plan, and watch Him do the impossible!

Daily Declaration

No matter what I'm facing today, I am coming through and out of it because My God is an odds-defying God, He knows my name and I am His favorite.

No Unmet Needs

"And my God will meet all your needs according to the riches of his glory in Christ Jesus."
– Philippians 4:19

Some of us are living in such a place of comfort that when things aren't going exactly the way we think that they should, we find ourselves complaining. Because we are accustomed to having certain things, we get all bent out of shape if things aren't perfect. Let's hereby deem today "No Complaints Day!"

Today serves as a reminder that no matter what it seems like we are lacking or how difficult things may be, God is still meeting our needs. He made a promise to never leave or forsake us, and He keeps that promise so well, that sometimes we fail to realize what He has done.

The Favor Factor

Even in the worst circumstance there is still a Favor Factor: God always provides. Thank God for that!

A lot of the things we say we "need" are really not needs. They are "wants." A need is a necessity. It's something we must have and can't live without. A need is food, but steak is a want. A need is shelter, but a four bedroom, two-story home is a want. Please understand that I'm not saying that we shouldn't desire certain things; I am saying that we shouldn't place those things in the "need" category and then become discouraged if we don't have them.

The Favor Factor

God's Word declares that He "shall" supply all of our needs. It doesn't say that He "might" supply them. It also says that He will supply "all" of our needs not "some." The things that we truly need, God has us covered. That's The Favor Factor; He will provide. But understand this, God will always take care of us, so the "needs" will always be met, but He never promised to give us everything that we want. That doesn't mean that we can't want things; it means that God will determine which of our wants are best for us. He'll also determine the best time for us to have them. Everything that we want isn't what's best for us, and just as a parent determines what's best for their child, our Father in Heaven does the same for us. But our needs are always covered, and that's favor.

Faith in Action

Let's just thank God for meeting all of our needs. Not according to our resources but according to His riches.

Day 13

I love that! Our needs are unequivocally met. We just use the term too loosely, and when we do that, it sets up room for discontentment. God opens and closes doors and makes ways for us every minute of the day and it's all for our good. Focus on those things, and trust with all of your heart that no matter what your current circumstance, it doesn't determine the final outcome! That's favor working for you!

Daily Declaration

Today and every day, my God will meet all my needs according to His riches in glory.

The Favor Factor

Don't Just Talk About It

"They claim to know God, but by their actions they deny him. They are detestable, disobedient and unfit for doing anything good." – Titus 1:16

MANY OF US HAVE THE "CHURCH" LINGO DOWN to a science. You know what I mean. If someone says to us, "How are you doing?" We answer, "Blessed and highly favored!" You know I'm right. And this, "when the praises go up," we answer right back, "blessings come down!" Then there is our favorite one, "God is good all the time;" and we say, "and all the time, God is good!"

Today let's talk about the idea of "practice what you preach." Understand this; actions will always speak louder than words. You can talk about who you are and what you stand for all day long, but if your actions don't align with what you are saying, it's all a lie. People, but most importantly God, hears your "lipping," but how are you really "living?"

The question is do we really believe these things we say? Are we really convinced that we are truly bless- ed and highly favored? Do we really believe that when we praise God, He inhabits the praise of His people? In those times of uncertainty when we don't know how things are going to work out, do we still believe that "God is still good?"

We can go on and on about how powerful and matchless God is with our mouths, but how are we liv- ing? What are we saying when we can't see the match- less and powerful work of God in our current storm? Are we still living as though He is good all the time? During a test or trial are we saying, "God will make a way" or "this too shall pass" but worry so much that it shows in every action?

This day is designed to encourage you to WALK THE TALK! Listen, you are blessed and not just favored, but HIGHLY favored. No matter what it looks like, God is a promise keeper! He promised to never leave nor forsake you, so act like you believe that!

The Favor Factor

Today's Favor Factor is knowing that you can rest in the assurance that as the favored of God, His word says He can and He WILL do what He says He will. . You must walk in the promises and principles that God has set before you. When God says you are a lender and not a borrower, but the credit report says otherwise, believe

Day 14

God! When He says you are the head and not the tail, but you feel like you are always left behind, trust God!

Faith in Action

Make up your mind right now that you will no longer just talk about His goodness, but that you will experience His goodness in the land of the living. Right here. Right now. You can now allow your mouth and your mind to be in sync with your heart. Walk the talk!

Daily Declaration

Today I will boldly walk the talk. My God is a promise keeper! He promised to never leave nor forsake me.

The Favor Factor

He's More Than
A Feeling

*"God is our refuge and strength, an ever-present help
in trouble." – Psalm 46:1*

NOW LET'S BE HONEST. SOMETIMES IT DOESN'T feel like God is with us. Very often this occurs when we become so distracted by the things that are important to us that we don't even recognize God's presence. It's usually not until our situation becomes desperate that we decide to call on God. After we've made a mess, then we decide we need to hear from God and then we invite Him into our circumstance. However, the truth is, God is always with us. He's waiting patiently for us to move out of the way and let Him take control.

Today I want to go ahead and clear one thing up.

The Favor Factor

Simply put, God is ALWAYS there! For years those of us who grew up in church or around "church folk" have heard or said this: "He may not come when you want Him, but He is always on time." Well, let's stop saying that right now. As of today, we will no longer say or live by those words because the Bible says that God is our refuge and strength, an ever-present (that means AL-WAYS present--current) help in trouble.

The Favor Factor

So here is The Favor Factor: when Jesus ascended up to heaven, one of the last statements that He made was that He is with us always. Did you catch that critical word? ALWAYS. Jesus did not say that He would be with us only when we recognize that we need Him. He didn't say that He would be with us only when we reach out to Him. He didn't say that He would be with us only after we make the right decisions. In Matthew 28:20, He says that He is with us always even until the end of the world. So why are we worrying about Him coming when we want Him? He promised to never leave us or forsake us; that's favor. Knowing that God is right there by my side, no matter what, is worth me waking up, getting out of bed, putting on my GOOD clothes, my GOOD shoes - hey ladies, some of us can even put on our GOOD hair - to represent Him every day. Whether it's a good day, bad day, trial, or triumph, we can have confidence that comes from knowing that through it all God is with me. You have favor all around you, on every side of you, covering you, protecting you, comforting you, and carrying you! How can you worry about anything when you know

Day 15

Who has your back?

Faith in Action

I dare you to wake up excited every morning to face new challenges, knowing that God will be right there with you every step of the way. That's favor!

Daily Declaration

Today, I'm not alone because my God is with me everywhere I go and He has my back. He will never leave or forsake me.

The Favor Factor

He's All You Need

"My grace is sufficient for you, for my power is made perfect in weakness. Therefore, I will boast all the more gladly about my weaknesses, so that Christ's power may rest on me. That is why, for Christ's sake, I delight in weaknesses, in insults, in hardships, in persecutions, in difficulties. For when I am weak, then I am strong." – 2 Corinthians 12:9-10

HAVE YOU EVER FELT DESPERATE? I MEAN REALLY, really desperate? I'm talking about days when you wake up and say, "I just can't do this life thing anymore." Have you had days when it seemed as though nothing is going the way you hoped? There is no way out of your situation? The money's not there, but even if was, it wouldn't fix your problems anyway. And just when you think that things can't get any worse, they do. When this happens you start to wonder if that breakthrough that you always heard about will ever come.

Today we focus on the true source of our strength—God.

I want you to know that I too have been there. I've felt like quitting. I've felt alone. I've even felt like life wasn't worth living, but I can also say that each and every time this has happened to me (I'm telling you what I know from experience), God has always come through. He has provided for me and my family in ways that it was undeniable that it was Him. In fact, I've learned that just when I think my situation is hopeless and every last resource has run out, THAT'S when God has operated in the most unimaginable ways.

The moment that you get ready to throw in the towel is the time to cry out to God. He is ready to trade His strength for your weakness. Look in the mirror and tell yourself that whatever I'm trying to do, God wants to do it bigger and better on my behalf.

Don't let the enemy bully you into thinking that it's over just because you can't do it on your own. Here's a newsflash; you aren't supposed to do it on your own anyway! What kind of parents would we be if we let our children constantly struggle without ever coming to their assistance? People would be ready to call the authorities on us for neglect, abuse, or unfit parenting if we saw our children suffer and never came to their aid. What kind of God would our God be if He treated us the same way?

Now think back for a minute about every time

that you thought you were too weak to make it. Obviously you made it because you are here, right? That's a "thank God moment" right there. Look at God's track record. If He was going to allow something to deplete you, He could have done that a long time ago. You've been through worse and you've made it. You've had other desperate times, but you made it. Guess what else? If you really think back and tell the truth about this thing, you also got a little bit stronger, better, wiser out of each of those desperate times. Now why in the world would God supply every need for you from birth until now just to leave you right here at this point? You have purpose, and you have ministry, and most importantly, you are a representation of God and responsible for drawing others to Him. If you give up, what kind of message are you sending about God's love, grace, and power?

The Favor Factor

The scripture lays it out plain and simple. God's grace is all that you need. God's grace gives you power when you don't feel it. It gives you strength when you don't sense it, and it gives you faith to believe against all odds. Yes, those things that you are dealing with SHOULD take you out, but The Favor Factor is that they CAN'T take you out because God is the source of your strength, He is the resource for everything that you need, and He is the peace to get you through until the manifestation of His promises come. Rest in the comfort of knowing that your resources are unlimited and God's glory will prevail.

Faith in Action

As Christians, God's glory should be evident in every aspect of our lives. That means the good, the bad and the ugly, because either way, the power of God will make us victorious. That's favor! The next time you are feeling weak, or going through, I challenge you to take a page from Paul's book, and begin to boast in the Lord so that Christ power can rest on you.

Daily Declaration

I will make it through this trial because God, You are strongest when I am weak and low. Today I will boast in You!

Count Your Blessings

"When you have eaten and are satisfied, praise the Lord your God for the good land he has given you."
— Deuteronomy 8:10

TODAY WE WILL FOCUS ON ACKNOWLEDGING GOD'S contributions to our lives. There was an old song that I used to sing at church when I was growing up that said, "Count your blessings, and name them one by one. Count your blessings, see what God has done." Now usually when we talk about counting our blessings, it's during a time when things aren't going our way and we are trying to remain grateful. If we are stuck in traffic, instead of complaining, we should think about how blessed we are that we have a car and aren't walking. If we aren't feeling well, we should consider that it's a blessing that we aren't as sick

The Favor Factor

as someone else. You get the picture. Traditionally, we count our blessings when things aren't going so well. I want to shift that way of thinking.

Consider today a reminder to count your blessings. Why do things have to be bad in order for us to acknowledge God? When things are not going our way, we find ourselves crying out to the Lord, "Help me God. Save me God. Fix it Jesus!" We ask others to pray for us, we come to church and listen to every word that the pastor says in hopes that it will get us closer to our breakthrough. But when things are going well, there's money in the bank, the kids are behaving, the spouse is affectionate, bills are paid, cars are in the driveway (you get the picture) – when everything is going well, sometimes we forget to acknowledge Christ the same way we did when we "needed" Him. Here's a word for you; we ALWAYS need God.

The Favor Factor

So as we count our blessings, let's do it at all times. Let's be honest, we aren't always "going through" difficulties. Sometimes we do actually go through seasons where everything is going well. The good days are really good, and we are actually happy. The Favor Factor is knowing beyond a shadow of doubt who the source of our happiness is. It is the favor of God resting on our lives, and allowing that season to take place. And, it's God's favor that turns a situation around for our good.

Let's start learning to count all the time. Let's acknowledge God's grace, mercy, and favor during the good times also. Thank you God for the routine exam where all the results came back normal. Thank you God for your child who graduated high school. Thank you God for my new promotion. Thank you God that I made it to and from my destination safely. There is no blessing too big or small that we can't acknowledge and thank God about.

Faith in Action

Let's begin today by practicing our counting. Each day, I challenge you to start your day by thanking God for as many things (tangible and intangible) that you can think of. I guarantee that doing this will set the tone for the rest of your day. Let's learn to count!

Daily Declaration

Today I will count my blessings and name them one by one. Thank You God for Your unmerited favor!

The Favor Factor

The Door Is Open, Your Move

"It is for freedom that Christ has set us free. Stand firm, then, and do not let yourselves be burdened again by a yoke of slavery." – Galatians 5:1

HAVE YOU EVER HEARD OF THE WORD RECIDIVISM? For those who haven't, it is a term used to describe the concept of repeated incarceration. It's when a person is released from prison after a long sentence, but after a very short period of time becomes incarcerated again. The person becomes so accustomed to being incarcerated that freedom becomes a challenge (for many different reasons) and they wind up back behind bars. Believe it or not that happens spiritually as well. We can become spiritually incarcerated, pray long and hard for God to release us, and when He does, we won't walk out into our freedom.

The Favor Factor

This day reminds us that we are free. God has delivered. Although we may not have reached our final destination, we are not in the same place that we started. Life sometimes causes us to feel incarcerated, but God does deliver. The problem is we become so accustomed to being behind bars, that when He opens the doors, we won't come out.

Take the children of Israel for example. They wandered around Egypt for 40 years! We'll just take that as a 40-year prison sentence because that would surely be classified as bondage. They could have been delivered long before that, but because of doubt and unbelief in God, they wandered and stayed in the same situation repeatedly until all of the unbelievers died. There were times when they were right at the border of the Promised Land, but because of doubt and complacency, they did not take hold of what God had for them.

Very often we blame the enemy for stuff that he's not even capable of doing. The enemy has no real power, and he certainly doesn't have any authority over us other than what we give him through fear, laziness, doubt, and flat out unbelief. God has flung the door wide open, but we don't walk through because we are afraid of what's on the other side.

God promised in Jeremiah that He only has plans to prosper us and not to harm us. Well, if God opened the door then surely there is nothing on the other side, but good. Deliverance is ready and waiting. God has the answers that you've been praying for, and the next chapter in your life has already been written. It's time to step into it. I'm going to mess somebody up right

Day 18

here. Freedom comes, not just from open doors, but from the doors that God shuts for us as well. Oops! I know that one stung a bit! Don't worry I'm preaching to myself too.

We've all heard it said that God will open doors that no man can shut and shut doors that no man can open. Well get this, the shut doors are also proof that you are favored. God shuts doors so that we can't go back to the way we used to be. He shuts them so that we have no choice but to accept our freedom. There are relationships that you want to go back to, but because you have the favor or God over your life, He won't allow it. There are places that you wanted to go, but God never allowed you to set foot back into those places that He delivered you from. God has set you free! You're out of jail, you're out of bondage, you are no longer a slave to your sin or circumstances; now operate in the new place that God has for you. Embrace the new you and new life in Christ that will be like nothing else that you have ever imagined.

The Favor Factor

The Favor Factor is that because you are the favored of God, He will keep you even when you don't want to be kept. He will protect you even when you don't know you need protecting. He will guide you when you feel like you have no direction and ALL of it will work for your good. Trust Him, and live like never before in the new place of peace, love, and freedom that God intended just for you.

Faith in Action

Think about the things that have been keeping you in bondage. Now decide that you will no longer be bound by those things, and declare your freedom in Jesus name.

Daily Declaration

Today I will not be held bound when God has set me free. I thank God for doors that have been opened and closed. I'm coming out with my hands up, thanking Him for His favor.

Know Your Assignment

"Submit yourselves, then, to God. Resist the devil, and he will flee from you." – James 4:7

LET'S AGREE ON ONE THING BEFORE WE MOVE ON. I hinted at this a little bit in Day 18, but I want to dive a bit more into it today. From now until Jesus comes and then after, let us stop using the devil as an excuse for the things that we do or don't do. It baffles me sometimes when I talk to people and they, as Christians, give the devil so much credit for the things that go wrong in their lives. You know what I mean; there are plenty of times I'm sure you've heard someone say, "The devil's been busy." Well the devil is just doing his job, no big deal. What WE should be doing now is our part.

The Favor Factor

This day focuses on the fact that as children of God we are set apart and have the ability to rise above adversity. Though it is tempting to give in to the negative forces around us, as disciples we are to be disciplined enough to set ourselves apart from these thoughts and actions. We represent Christ, and when we do this, we stand out as His children.

Back in the 70's, there was a comedian by the name of Flip Wilson who developed the catch phrase "the devil made me do it." Basically, according to Flip, anything mischievous that happened was caused by the devil. Well at least we know that Flip Wilson's skit was intended for comic relief, but what's our excuse? We do the same thing that Flip Wilson did, only he was joking and we absolutely stand by our "blame game."

As I said before, we know that the devil is on his job to steal, kill, and destroy, but what about our job? Our job as Christians is to draw all men to Christ. We are supposed to do this by being living and breathing examples of Christ. Everything that Christ had, He left with us when He ascended to Heaven. He left us power, authority, and dominion and an all access pass to Him if we need a little recharge along the way. Well, if this is the case, then why are we, Christians, sometimes the biggest complainers and whiners that you will find.

Sometimes we can act so defeated that it seems like we forget whose we are. Why blame everything on the devil and even tell others how busy the devil is in our lives when we were assigned to emphasize and demon- strate the goodness of God to everyone we meet? The devil might be busy, but GOD is always busier. He is a

Day 19

God who never sleeps nor slumbers. He is always on the case. We also have Jesus, the intercessor that came down to earth and showed us firsthand how to overcome adversity.

Today's scripture reminds us to first submit ourselves to God. Submit means to totally yield over to God. Since we are submitting to God, that means when we have problems, (and we will) trials, and tests, we can go to God with them, and He will direct us each time. Since our job is to consult and commune with Christ, we should be growing in our faith, power, and endurance.

Luke 10:19 clearly says, "I have given you authority to trample on snakes and scorpions and to overcome all the power of the enemy; nothing will harm you." That scripture, plus our main scripture for the day, should be all that we need to realize that what God has for us, no one, not even the devil, can take away. Jesus said that NOTHING would harm you. He said that we could defeat the enemy. This is a fixed fight. Go into it knowing that you have already won. That means whatever the devil tries to make you do, you have the power to overcome it; you just have to use it.

The Favor Factor

The Favor Factor is we are the ones who have the all-access pass to victory. Like I said previously, you are free! Walk in your freedom. As of today we will no longer allow the enemy to bully us. We will walk into each battle knowing that we have already won, and we will utilize the power and authority that we have been given to show the world just how busy God is in our lives.

Faith in Action

Beginning today, refuse to give the enemy credit for anything in your life, and instead declare your victory in Christ Jesus.

Daily Declaration

I am a child of God and I am victorious! Today I rise against adversity that comes against me with the power and authority given to me. Today and every day I am a winner!!

It's Time To Focus On The "But"

"But those who hope in the LORD will renew their strength. They will soar on wings like eagles; they will run and not grow weary, they will walk and not be faint." – Isaiah 40:31

L ET ME PAINT A FEW PICTURES FOR YOU. HAVE YOU EVER worked for something only to be disappointed after all of your hard work because you were still unable to attain it? Are you a single man or woman, waiting for Mr. or Miss Right, only to constantly end up with Mr. or Miss Wrong? Have you asked the Lord how many more weddings and baby showers before it's my own? Do you work two and three jobs to BARELY pay your bills? Are you always on the go but never see the fruit of your labor and efforts? Are your children going astray despite your every effort to pray for them and help them? Oh, I can go on and on, but the point is we all have things that we have worked for and found ourselves on the verge of giving up because we don't see the fruit of our labor.

Today we will shift our focus and concentrate on those things that God has promised to us. This day will be a game changer for us all … a shift will take place. We will commit to a change in our actions, thoughts, and deeds. Today is the day that we focus on the but!

Be honest; you are tired and worn out, and just trying to figure out when this breakthrough that you hear so many testifying about going to come. When is it your turn? Well, today is a new day. You will no longer let your current circumstances cause doubt to creep into your mind. Today, instead of focusing on the problems, we are going to focus on the BUT.

In Isaiah 40:31, the "but" cancels out everything else that was previously said. It is basically saying despite all that was mentioned before, THEY (the favored of God) that wait upon the Lord shall renew their strength. Oh my goodness, there is so much to say about just that one line. The first word they, indicates that there is a distinction between those who were mentioned before the "but" and after the "but." Those who came before the, "but" were tired, weary, and stumbling, BUT (there's that word again) THEY that wait upon the Lord SHALL renew their strength.

Let's not skip over the word WAIT. This is the word that we who live in this instant society dread hearing but it's inevitable. Sometimes we just have to wait, and that even applies to the favored. This scripture is saying, yes, you are different, but you will also have to wait on the Lord. It's telling us that when we do wait, we will gain the strength to endure, even when we feel like giving up. We need to recognize that there are some things that aren't going to adhere to our personal time-lines. That baby may come at 36 rather than 30, that job may come after the 12th interview rather than the 2nd; that healing may come after a few more therapy treatments or even a few more relapses. Whatever the time-line, focus on the fact that waiting on the Lord builds strength, and as the scripture says, it SHALL (meaning it's inevitable) happen.

The Favor Factor

Everyone at some point or another has times when they feel like giving up, but the difference between you and everybody else is that you are NOT everybody else. You have favor over your life. It is The Favor Factor that sets you apart from others but also draws others to you, and ultimately to Christ. I remember hearing people say "when they could've lost their minds," God kept them. He has done it for so many others, and He will do the same for you. So remember, you are favored. You can endure. You can celebrate a few more baby showers, you can go on a few more job interviews and you can suffer a few more disappointments because you are favored and you will be renewed.

Faith in Action

Imagine the response if people see your challenges but also see your peace while enduring them. That's a surefire way to get people interested in Christ. You are saying to everyone that "despite what you have seen me endure, I am stronger and I'm waiting patiently on the Lord because I know that He will take care of me." Let's put it in action!

Daily Declaration

I will wait on the Lord and He will renew my strength. I will soar on wings like eagles; run and not grow weary, walk and not faint.

He Can Use You Anyway

"*Then Joshua son of Nun secretly sent two spies from Shittim. 'Go, look over the land,' he said, 'especially Jericho.' So they went and entered the house of a prostitute named Rahab and stayed there.*"
— *Joshua 2:1*

Have you ever done something that you are ashamed of? Have you done anything that you know was not pleasing to God? Maybe you were addicted to drugs; or maybe you have cheated on your spouse, or were convicted of a crime. You may have lied, stolen, or maybe even worse. I know that we all have had days when we didn't make the best decisions. As much as you try to put the past in the past and move forward, there is always someone who finds great pleasure in reminding you of your past. No matter how determined you may be to move forward, experience has shown me that there are always people who reconvict you over and over for your crimes. These are what I call the "remember when" people. Well today, I want to encourage you to keep pushing forward despite the "remember when" people. Let me tell you this, no matter what you used to do, God is still ready to use you now for His greater good.

Today we will be reminded that God can still use us for His glory no matter how dirty, unworthy, or used up we may think we are.

I like Rahab because she was the underdog. She was the least regarded, but she made the biggest impact. She is also the one that no one counted on but the one who counted the most. You see, Rahab was a prostitute, and not only was she living that lifestyle, everyone in the town knew about it. Think about it; this was a small town, everyone knew each other, everyone talked to each other. They knew where Rahab's house was, they saw the men come and go from her house; they probably heard and told the stories of what went on in the house. Her sins were definitely exposed and so she was labeled, judged, and isolated because of her "profession." I am sure that you can imagine the way she was treated because it was probably no differently than we treat people today. Today with social media, camera phones, gossip sites and every other piece of technology, the word about the latest scandal travels fast, and we all become the judge and jury for the prosecuted.

It was no different for Rahab. She was known as Rahab, the Harlot and people probably expected very little from her. Since she was a prostitute she was most likely viewed as used, trashy, low class, and unworthy of respect. However, what she had that was more valuable than anything else was her faith. Before the Battle of Jericho, Joshua sent two spies into the city but if they were identified, which was close to happening, they would be captured and killed. Not only that, if the king knew that Rahab was helping them, she too could be killed. Rahab had a purpose, she was an essential part of God's plan and even as a prostitute she was vital to God's plan.

The other part that I like about Rahab is that she knew how important she was to the mission. She recognized that she was needed by God, even though she was a sinner. What I want you to understand today is that even though others may feel that you are useless because of your shortcomings, God recognizes your worth. He believes in you, and He knows that there is more to you than your sin. No, he doesn't want you to stay in sin, but what I love about God is that even in your sin, you are useful to Him. Rahab was not a reformed prostitute when God used her; she was right in the thick of her lifestyle when God used her for His greater purpose.

The Favor Factor

I want you to remember that although people may only see your shortcomings, God sees something more. Here is The Favor Factor, God values you, and you are useful to Him and the Kingdom no matter what anyone else thinks. He wants you right where you are. Let me give you an example of how useful Rahab went on to be: she is an ancestor of Jesus. So allow God to have His way with you. You are called for a greater purpose. Here we go; you are FAVORED by God. Don't get it twisted; God knew that Rahab was a prostitute. He knew everything about her. In fact, He knew that she would be a prostitute before she was even a prostitute. The same way that God favored Rahab, He favors you. Get ready to be used in the best way!

Faith in Action

Has God called you for a greater purpose but you discounted it because you didn't feel worthy? He knows who you are and what you've done, and He still chose you … so just say, "yes."

Daily Declaration

My past doesn't matter to God, my Father. I am loved and valuable. I was specifically designed and chosen for a special work.

Living My Best Life

"The thief comes only to steal and kill and destroy; I have come that they may have life, and have it to the full." – John 10:10

TODAY'S MESSAGE IS SIMPLE. GET BUSY AND LIVE your best life! God is always protecting and watching over us, so even when things do get tough, I like to think of it as God allowing me to represent Him in the best way during the worst times. I believe He has so much faith in me to defeat the adversity that He gives the devil permission to attack me because He knows that in the end, I'm going to allow Him to fight the battle that will ultimately give Him the glory. It is all part of God's plan.

You know that we were put here to worship God and to give Him all the glory in everything we do, right?

The Favor Factor

We are also supposed to be examples of Christ and through that example we are to draw people to Him. If someone sees us trust God through adversity, they will trust God with their own situations when they face difficult times. Giving credit to the devil takes the focus off of God. The Bible tells us that when we keep our minds on Christ, He will give us peace, and that's even through turbulent situations.

The Favor Factor

Even as it relates to today's scripture, people will say, "Yeah the devil is busy. You know he comes to steal, kill, and destroy." What? And? That's not the end of that scripture. Part B of that scripture says, "I (Jesus) have come that they may have life and have it to the full." Now that's The Favor Factor, the King James Version that says, "I come that they might have life more abundantly!" In other words, nothing that the devil tries to do is of consequence, and it certainly won't prevail because God favors you.

I can think of many times that I've watched people overcome so many obstacles with such grace and faith that even I was in awe of their relationship with Christ. During those times, their example motivated me to get closer to God so that when it's my turn, I can handle the situation with the same faith. That's the point of your trial. It's not for you, it's for someone else. God favored you to experience your trial because He had faith that you would handle it in a Godly manner and draw others through it. Remember that you are favored and focus more on God than the problem.

Day 22

So now:

If the light bill is overdue say, "God is my provider."
If the house is foreclosed say, "God is my shelter."
If a loved one dies say, "God is my comforter."
If a coworker is difficult say, "God is my peace."
If faced with sickness say, "God is my healer."

Focusing on Christ gives us the power to sustain during the trial; it rejuvenates us. We gain a renewed strength by focusing on Jesus. So take the attention off of the devil, whether he is busy or not, he is a loser and he won't win. God, however, will always prevail.

Faith in Action

Beginning today, determine that you won't give the devil credit for anything but will instead give God the glory. You are favored for a greater purpose; let God get the glory because He deserves it.

Daily Declaration

Today I will focus on the Problem Fixer instead of the problem. He is my provider, shelter, comforter, healer and peace. He enables me to live my best life!

The Favor Factor

Someone Is Assigned To You

"When Elizabeth heard Mary's greeting, the baby leaped in her womb, and Elizabeth was filled with the Holy Spirit. - Luke 1:41

'VE NOTICED THROUGHOUT MY LIFE THAT WHENEVER I HAVE a pivotal moment, God sends just the right people to help and support me through it. There is an old saying that some people are in your life for a lifetime, while some are there only for a season. Whichever time slot the person is allotted, just know that God favors you so much that He allows individuals to go through your exact same experience just so they can help you when it was your turn. The experience doesn't have to be bad; it can be a new baby, purchasing a house for the first time, choosing a college, or anything else but I can almost guarantee that whatever milestone you have experienced there has been someone who assisted you through it in some capacity. That person was assigned to your team.

I really want to encourage you today and let you know that you are not alone. Yes, you have our Father in Heaven who will never leave you or forsake you, but He has also placed people here on earth specifically designated as your support system throughout every part of your life.

You don't have to deal with anything on your own. First of all, God can speak to you directly but also because He knows that we sometimes waiver in our faith, He sends people as confirmation of what He has spoken to us. I know that when times seem tough or situations get a bit overwhelming. You may feel like you are the only one going through your trial and sometimes you just want to be alone and handle things yourself. But remember this, life is not a competition but you do have a team. There's always someone who can help guide you through the best and worst of times. Because God favors you so much no matter what type of situation, He has designated earthly support just for you.

The story of Mary and Elizabeth provides the perfect example of feeling alone and finding someone who is on your team. When the angel of the Lord told Mary that she was pregnant with Jesus, she was probably a little surprised by the news. She had to deal with a lot. First of all, she was a young girl, she was a virgin, she was engaged, she was well known, and she would be the mother of Jesus Christ. That's quite a bit to handle all at once, right?

Think about the constant attention that celebrities face now in both their personal and professional lives. And though Mary was not a "celebrity," news such as hers would be the talk of the town. So Mary, who probably felt very alone at the time, traveled to see her cousin Elizabeth who believed her, encouraged her, and reassured her that what was happening to her was indeed of God and for a far greater purpose than she could imagine.

Not only was Elizabeth able to comfort Mary based on her own faith in God but also because the same thing was happening to her. She too was pregnant and under very complicated circumstances. Elizabeth was much older and had given up hope of having children, but the same angel of the Lord came to her and told her that she was pregnant and confirmed with her that Mary was pregnant. Talk about a good team member! God orchestrated that perfectly for Mary. Just when she had probably given up any hope that anyone would believe her, let alone understand her situation, God sent her to the one other person who knew exactly what was happening because she too was having the same experience.

The Favor Factor

Just like Mary, you too are highly favored, and God is also with you. The Favor Factor is that God has assigned people like Elizabeth to stand with you here on earth to hold you accountable to His will for your life. Isn't that just amazing? Saying that you are blessed and highly favored isn't just a church-folk slogan that we say after being greeted; it's the truth.

Today I encourage you to be confident, be blessed, and know that you are not alone and that God has assigned someone specifically for you who will confirm in your spirit those things that He has already spoken.

Faith in Action

God favors you for a very special assignment that only you can fulfill. Trust in His plan and watch Him work.

Daily Declaration

Today, I say yes to Your will, and direction. I except my assignment and will boldly go and do as You say because I trust Your plan, and know that I'm never alone.

Keeping Up
With Christ

"Your word is a lamp for my feet, a light on my path."
— Psalm 119:105

HAVE YOU EVER HAD YOUR DAY, WEEK, YEAR, OR LIFE turned completely upside down? Have you ever had something totally blindside you to the point that you just have no idea how you will get through it?

Today serves as a reminder that although situations may catch you off guard, they weren't unexpected to God. He already knew your every problem, victory, and circumstance. The great part about all of this is, not only did He know about it, but He also already has it worked out. God ordained this great book called The Holy Bible that has a solution for every possible situation that you can imagine. He loves us so much that He has put everything in one place to make sure that we can navigate through this adventure that we call life.

If you find yourself uneasy, worried, or anxious, just flip on over to Isaiah 26:3 where we are reminded that God will keep us in perfect peace if we keep trusting in Him. If you are faced with sickness, Isaiah 53 helps you to understand that we are healed by the stripes of Jesus. There will be times when you feel rejected, disappointed, and uncertain, but God provides assurance in Jeremiah when He says, "For I know the plans I have for you, plans to prosper you and not to harm you, plans to give you hope and a future."

So what's my point? It's simple; look to God for the answers, the comfort, the healing, and the peace that you are searching for. He has provided every single thing we need to be successful and satisfied in this life through His Word. So often we run to every other source for guidance rather than running to the One who is the ultimate guide.

Psalms 119: 105 brilliantly illustrates the majesty of God's Word. It is described as a light, and lights magnify and illuminate. Where light is present, darkness is absent. That means that when we immerse ourselves in the Word of God, it removes the darkness so that we are no longer lost. The Word of God guides us and it also saves us. Everything that you need is found in the Word of God. As I mentioned before, we tend to go out of our way to find solutions for life's circumstances.

The Favor Factor

Here's The Favor Factor. God favors us, His children, so much that He has provided a very detailed instruction manual to guide us through life. Now the majority of us don't read the instruction manual for anything else. We "test" it through trial and error; we watch videos and snippets on social media, but we don't take the time to really learn the specific details of our new product. But the minute something goes wrong, we search through the instruction manual desperate to find the answers. Just as with the instruction manual to our cars, gadgets, products, or appliances, certain issues can be avoided beforehand, if we would only proactively read our manual (the Bible).

Faith in Action

I challenge you today to read your manual, trust God, and pray; you are favored, and God is waiting with open arms to bear your burdens and direct your path. I promise you will NOT be disappointed.

Daily Declaration

Today I commit to reading and learning the instruction manual so that I can stand ready with answers as I face life's ups and downs.

The Favor Factor

A Greater Call

"The LORD does not look at the things people look at. People look at the outward appearance, but the LORD looks at the heart." – 1 Samuel 16:7

Most of us have been overlooked many times in life for many different opportunities. You may feel like nothing will ever work in your favor and that perhaps even God, Himself has overlooked you. We've all been labeled by people for things that we've done, or even worse, things that we didn't do. The great thing about having a relationship with God is that we can rely on Him to know who we are.

Today, I want you to remember this: it doesn't matter how you look to people; God has a greater calling for you.

The Favor Factor

There are so many instances in the Bible where men and women of God were given a label by the world but called something different by God. David was called "ruddy". He was a murderer, an adulterer. But to God he was a king, a man after God's own heart. When the world declared that Abraham and Sarah were too old to have children, God called them to be parents. He called Abraham to be the father of many nations. I want you to realize today that no matter what the world calls you, God has called you for a specific purpose. He is not concerned about your shortcomings. He knows about all of our faults and flaws. The great thing about God is that He knows about them and He still loves us.

Let's look at an example of this in the Bible. When God called Moses to save his people, Moses pushed back. Moses told God that he couldn't do what was being asked of him because he had a speech impediment; as if God didn't already know this! Moses said "I am slow of speech and tongue." God responded in Exodus 4:11 by saying "Who gave man his mouth? Who makes him deaf or mute? Who gives him sight or makes him blind? Is it not I, the Lord? Now go. I will help you speak and will teach you what to say." God is saying to you I know that you may not speak or dress properly. I know that you may not have the right education. I certainly know that you have a past, but go anyway! Do as He tells you to because He will equip you with the ability to speak, dress, and mingle in any environment. No matter your shortcomings, God will more than make up for your lack of ability. Just go forth and do what He asks. That is the power of God's favor. He will make our less than, more than enough!

The Favor Factor

God is asking you to do these things because He knows the stuff you are made of. Although, you alone are not capable, because of who you are, you can do all things through Christ. You may be asking "who am I?" If I'm not all those things that the world says I am, then who exactly am I? Your Father calls you son or daughter. And since you are sons and daughters of God, who is the Most High King, this means that you are princes and princesses. Yes, you are royalty! How about that Favor Factor? You are meant to inherit the riches of His Kingdom. Because of your status you also have access to everything in God's arsenal to enable you to live out the calling that has been placed on your life.

You may have been called something other than your name for many years. You may have even gotten used to being exactly what the world has declared you to be. How have all those labels worked out for you? If I had to take a guess, I'd say they haven't helped. The only way that you will know and understand who God has called you to be is if you first know what God calls you.

This is what God calls you:

Fearfully and wonderfully made (Psalms 139:14)
An Incredible work of art (Ephesians 2:10)
Loved and chosen by God (1 Thessalonians 1:4)
A joint-heir with Christ (Romans 8:17)

Faith in Action

It is time to begin to declare and believe what God says about you. It's time to toss out every single label that has ever hindered you from realizing the call that God has on your life. When Satan tries to tell you who you are through lies and deception, use these verses to speak the truth about who you are. God has called you so many wonderful things. Align yourself with His word so that you can to begin to understand and know who He has called you to be.

Daily Declaration

I am who God says I am. I am fearfully and won-derfully made, an incredible work of art, loved and chosen by God, a joint-heir with Christ. I am MORE than a Conqueror!

The Power Of A Closed Mouth

"And to aspire to live quietly, and to mind your own affairs, and to work with your hands, as we instructed you, so that you may walk properly before outsiders and be dependent on no one."
— 1 Thessalonians 4:11-12

HOW MANY TIMES HAVE WE SPOKEN WHEN GOD HAS clearly told us to be quiet? How many times have we meddled in others' affairs when we knew it was none of our business? I can say with great certainty that if you've lived for more than a couple of decades, then you have encountered both situations.

Today we will focus on the power of keeping quiet and letting God work. When we speak on things without confirmation from God, we open the door for arguments and strife in our lives and in relationships. When we take on other people's problems or poke our nose in where it doesn't belong, we make a choice to try to fix someone else's situation rather than letting God do His work.

The bottom line today is that sometimes we just have to keep quiet and mind our own business. This is especially true when we encounter situations that we feel strongly about. Maybe we have an issue with our spouse or friend, and we just have to let them know right now! We think "Well bless God; they aren't going to treat me like this!" So instead of taking the situation (and our anger) to God, we decide to handle it ourselves. Let me tell you that handling it yourself is going to end up with one or more parties feeling upset or one person admitting (but not totally agreeing) to who is right in the matter. These types of encounters can ruin a relationship, leaving everyone feeling offended and the issue still unresolved. Sometimes we even go a bit further, offering advice or help in matters that simply do not concern us. It is during these times that we often discover that we have not helped at all, but made things worse.

The negative outcome of these types of circumstances is not a coincidence. When we interfere or pry when God has not told us to, we will encounter problems. You may be thinking that you didn't hear from God on whether or not you should've said anything. In those cases, be quiet! If God has not told you to speak or intervene in a matter, then you should say and do nothing. God wants us to live quietly so that He can

Day 26

work. Before we speak, maybe God needs to soften the person's heart so that they can receive the message. Or maybe God wants us to calm down and realize that what we are upset about is really not that serious. Or even better, God wants that person to know who He is. God may want to perform the miraculous, and by being obedient, we leave no doubt as to Who deserves the glory.

The Bible tells us that the power of life and death is in the tongue. Therefore, we know that what comes from our mouths has the power to build up the Kingdom or the power to help the enemy destroy it. A closed mouth can be extremely powerful especially when we refuse to engage in conversations rooted in gossip, malice, or those that are burdensome to others. Remaining quiet in these times can show others who we are as Christians. We are in the business of doing God's business, and this entails staying focused on the work He wants us to do.

Many times in the scripture we are told to be silent, calm, gentle. It takes strength to remain hushed when our flesh wants us to speak. Those who always have something to say and have no control over their mouth are not powerful. In fact, they are powerless and foolish. You and I both know that sometimes we have to bite our tongue, lip, or cheek to stop ourselves from saying the wrong things! If it were so easy to remain quiet, then we wouldn't have to go to such measures to guard our mouths and the words that come from it. God wants us to be meek and even-tempered, busy working so that we are not caught up in anything slanderous to others and certainly not to His Kingdom. In doing so we present to the world a worthy depiction of what it means to be a Christian. It's never too late to practice keeping our mouths closed and busying ourselves with the work that God has put before us.

The Favor Factor

The Favor Factor is we have been given the grace needed to understand there is a time for everything, even as it relates to our speech. Our focus should always be to let our speech be seasoned so that we will know how and when to speak. Watch your mouth.

Faith in Action

You can start today. Keep busy and stay the course that God has set forth for you. Listen to the gentle nudge of the Holy Spirit telling you when to stay quiet and when to speak. Pray to God for guidance on when you should intercede. I promise you your request for direction will not be in vain. God listens and He will answer.

Daily Declaration

Today I will watch my mouth. I will be quick to listen, slow to speak, and slow to become angry.

Your Name Is Servant

"Sitting down, Jesus called the Twelve and said,
'Anyone who wants to be first must be the very last,
and the servant of all.'" – Mark 9:35

WHEN YOU THINK ABOUT JESUS CHRIST WHAT comes to mind? Is it the countless miracles that He performed? His ability to heal the sick? His meek and humble spirit? Or His sacrifice on the cross? No matter what image of Christ comes to mind, all of them should paint a picture of a Man who was a servant to the people. If Christ, the son of God, could come to earth and serve mankind, then we as Christians (Christ-like people) should be able to serve as well. The example that God sent for us is yet another Favor Factor. We should fall to our knees and thank God for such a perfect and living

The Favor Factor

model of how to live our lives.

Today we will focus on servitude. No title is greater to God than "servant." If we have not led someone to Christ or been a servant of the kingdom, then we have not served our purpose.

The Favor Factor

Even though Jesus is God himself in human form, He made it a point to serve others. He tells us in today's scripture that if we want to be first, we must be last; a servant to all. This means that God does not look at the worldly definition of success! In the world we are great because of our accomplishments, money, power even education. It doesn't matter if we have mistreated people, if we have been immoral in our quest to seek success. The world defines success based on what we accomplish here. However, God looks at those who serve as the most successful, the greatest. It is only through serving others that we can be a light in a dark world, showing others the love of Christ and leading them to the kingdom. The Favor Factor is that we don't have to measure up to the world's standards to be successful in God's view.

Jesus and His disciples went around serving others. Because they put others needs above their own, they left a lasting mark on society. Serving has somehow taken on a negative connotation even though Christ Himself was the greatest servant of all. Think about how much of an impact you can have on the lives of others if you take the time to meet their needs. A single mom who is overwhelmed with bills and kids could use some-

Day 27

one with a servant's mentality to offer a couple hours of free childcare. A senior citizen who is bed-ridden may need a person with a servant's spirit to take care of their grocery shopping or help them clean up. You see, it's not the people who go through life thinking only of themselves that bring others to the Kingdom, it's those who are willing to step out of their comfort zone to help others that really make an impact. When someone is down and out they will remember the selfless person who always make themselves available. They will wonder how you can keep going, how in the midst of all that is going on in the world, you are able to continue to be so giving. And when they reach the point where they are seeking and asking you how or why, this is the time when you share your testimony of what Christ has done for you and let them know that the Savior is ready and willing to do the same for them

Over the years Christians have used their religion as a whip. Constantly telling people all the things they are doing wrong. Did you know that minister and serve are synonyms? That means that as ministers of God, which we all are, we are called "to serve" God. However, we want to be served as if we are in a secret club that no one else is privy to. That is not how God wants us to be! God wants us to share His love in hopes that we will bring others to Him. His desire is that none shall perish! And therefore He has given us an accurate depiction of what it takes to lead others to Him. We have to give them Jesus, and the only way to do this is by serving them. Jesus, who was without blame, made Himself a servant to sinners. He knew that humbling Himself and presenting Himself as a living sacrifice was part of fulfilling the prophecy to save mankind. By doing so He changed countless lives.

Faith in Action

Anyone of us who follows Christ should be able to do the same. As believers, our purpose is to be servants of the Kingdom and lead people to Christ. Take time out to do something for someone that demonstrates a servant's heart today.

Daily Declaration

Today, I will share the love of Jesus with someone by serving. Lord, help me to humble myself and have a servant's heart.

Simply Trust

*"'For my thoughts are not your thoughts, neither are
your ways my ways,' declares the LORD."*
– Isaiah 55:8

ET'S GET ONE THING CLEAR TODAY: NEITHER YOU
nor I am God. God is infinite, all-powerful, and
all-knowing. Our bodies are finite, our knowledge limited, and our power is only magnified
to the extent that we are willing to trust and rely on God.
If everything that I mentioned is the case, why then do
we seek to understand God, when our ability to do so
is severely restricted? We can never know the thoughts
and ways of God because everything about Him is on
a higher level than we can ever perceive. The sooner
we realize that, the easier our journey with Him will become.

The Favor Factor

Even though we strive to be Christ-like, we must understand that we will never be perfect. Not only is God perfect; God is. You only have to look at who we are and who He is to know why His thoughts are different from ours. We are sin-filled creatures; God is without sin. We have the ability to lie and deceive. God cannot lie. Our capacity to love can be hindered by our emotions. God's love is unconditional. Our ability to affect others is restricted by geographical location and our own selfishness. God's impact is boundless, vast, and selfless, and He is concerned about each and every one of us. I draw such a stark comparison between us and the Father so that you can grasp the fact that His ways are higher than ours. Therefore, His thoughts are higher than anything we can ever comprehend.

The Favor Factor

This brings me to my point today. Since God's thoughts and ways are beyond our comprehension, then we need to realize that our job as believers is not to understand but to simply trust Him. Trust that because He is our Father and knows better than we do what's best for us, that He is working things out in our favor. There goes that word again: favor. The Favor Factor comes into play because despite the fact that our thoughts don't always align with His, He still makes a way for us. His favor on our lives is working things out for our good even though we have done nothing to earn it. God tells us that all things work out for those of us who love Him and are called according to His purpose. God says all, not some. This promise means that God's thoughts include a purpose for you.

We've mentioned Jeremiah 29:11 before, but it bears repeating. The scripture says "I know the plans I have for you." We get frustrated because the plans we make don't work out. But did you consult God before you made those plans? The plans we make all by ourselves may not be the plans that God has for us. The thoughts we have about who we are and our calling may not align with the thoughts that God has about us. We may not understand everything that happens in our lives but we must trust that it all has divine purpose. God has already made a plan for us and nothing we can do will sway God's calling on our life.

Faith in Action

His thoughts are more righteous and immeasurably higher than ours. Today trust that He knows best, that His thoughts include plans for you to have a hopeful future, His favor shows up in all kinds of ways in our lives.

Daily Declaration

Your thoughts are higher than mine so Father today and every day, I will trust You.

The Favor Factor

Love Them Anyway

"But I tell you, love your enemies and pray for those who persecute you." – Matthew 5:44

I CAN IMAGINE YOUR REACTION TO TODAY'S MESSAGE. As you're reading this, you may be screaming "but you don't know what they did to me!" You may be filled with so much hurt or anger because you were wronged. Although that hurt and anger may be justified, holding on to it is not. God wants us to have an abundant life, one in which we receive His favor with open arms. We can't live an abundant life if we are empty and bitter inside. We cannot receive God's favor with open arms if our arms are filled with all the burdens we carry because of what someone has done to us. God wants us to be free; free to live out that life He has planned for

The Favor Factor

us. We can only do this through the power of love.

Today's message is a tough one – even for me – but it is so important. We will focus on loving those who spitefully use you. We will learn to tap into the power of love and forgiveness that Christ has given us to live a life free from hate and blame.

God wants us to love. He loves us and in His infinite wisdom has not only instructed us to do so, but shows us through Jesus Christ how to live a life of love. Love is not discriminatory. When God tells us to love, He does so without restriction. This means that we are not only to love those who work with us, but also to love those who work against us; those who have conspired to do us wrong; those who may have purposely hurt us. God doesn't want us to turn away from them or to show them malice. He wants us to love them. In fact, I believe He wants us to love the hell out of them! What I mean by this is we should display so much love towards them that we thwart any attempt that the devil may have of sending them to hell.

Don't you see? When we choose to forgive others, we acknowledge the goodness of God while at the same time halting the efforts of the enemy. When people are spiteful and wicked, they are being used by the enemy. Many times they do not even realize that they are being used. They have not connected their greed, jealousy, and ill-intents against you to the malevolent one. It is the devil that we should war against, not our fellow man. The Bible tells us that our fight is not against flesh and blood but against the powers of darkness (Ephesians 10:12). We must understand that when we choose to love our enemies instead of hating them, to pray for them instead of cursing them, then we are using the power that God has given us to fight against evil forces.

Not only do we stop any plans that the enemy has by using love as a shield, but we also lighten our burden as well. It is hard to stay mad at someone! When you decide to stay mad at someone then you allow yourself to continually focus or meditate on the reason why you're angry. Meditating on the situation will only cause those feelings of anger, hurt, and betrayal to grow and become deeply rooted in your mind and spirit. You develop a spirit of bitterness that can have a physical and mental effect on you. Being bitter may cause you to have a physical reaction to the person you're mad at. When you are in close quarters with them your heart may start to beat faster and you may feel yourself starting to get stressed out. All of this occurs because you have allowed bitterness to fester and take root in your life. Let it go!

Holding on to anger and unforgiveness only allows the enemy to work in your life. If you hold on to it, you let him win! There is a reason why the Bible tells us not to let the sun go down on our anger. Doing so just allows it to fester and grow until we eventually sin ourselves. And that is just what the enemy wants. He wants us bogged down by resentment and rage towards our enemies so that God's favor can't show up in our lives. It's not worth it. The anger, no matter how justified, you have for a person is not worth losing out on all the things God has for you.

The Favor Factor

The Bible tells us to forgive, over and over again. There is no limit to how many times we can forgive. Every time we are wronged, we can, and should forgive. The Favor Factor is that God favors us and has given us an immeasurable capacity to forgive because that is the essence of who He is and what He does. We aren't able to love and forgive on our own. Today I want you to know that you are more than a conqueror through Jesus Christ because He loves you!

Faith in Action

Tap into that love and favor that He has for you by connecting with Him in prayer. Pray for those who have wronged you. You can intervene for them by asking God to open their eyes and change their hearts. Pray for yourself, asking for a better attitude and a forgiving heart. In the process you will find that He is also changing you. The more you pray, the easier it becomes to forgive.

Daily Devotion

I refuse to let the sun go down on my wrath. Right now, I let go of all unforgiveness and bitterness, and today I pray for my enemies.

The Glory From Your Story

"You have never been tempted to sin in any different way than other people. God is faithful. He will not allow you to be tempted more than you can take. But when you are tempted, He will make a way for you to keep from falling into sin." – 1 Corinthians 10:13

I F EVEN JESUS HIMSELF WAS TEMPTED, WHY ARE YOU surprised by the temptations that come your way? It is not God who tempts us to sin. We do not serve a schizophrenic God who roots for our success one day and then wishes for our demise the next. No, our God is the same. He always tells the truth, He always loves, and His promises are meant to be fulfilled if we do our part.

Today we will learn to appreciate the "story" and understand what God has in store for you through your story. You were specifically chosen to go through your story so that God can get the glory out of it. What happened to you wasn't for you; it wasn't even about you, but God favored you out of everyone else to deal with it because He trusted you to come through and out.

The Bible says that we have all sinned and fallen short of God's glory (Romans 3:23). Our mistakes, our trials, our tests come together to form our testimony. As Christians each and every one of us has a story to tell. It is our declaration of the goodness of God in our lives. Our stories serve as evidence that we have witnessed the glorious favor of God. When we have gone through something we have an obligation to share our story so that those who are wavering will know that there is hope; no matter the situation, if we hold fast to God, then His favor will bring us through.

God will however let us go through hardships. These hardships are not meant to destroy us but are designed to help mold us into the person that God wants us to be. He can't use us when we are bogged down with stuff. This "stuff" may be bad habits, haughty attitudes, or an inability to forgive. We may be held back by the type of people we deal with, the sort of business we involve ourselves in, or even the kind of mindset we have.

Let's look to 2 Corinthians 4:7-9 for a better depiction of this process: "But we have this treasure in jars of clay to show that this all-surpassing power is from God and not from us. 8 We are hard pressed on every side, but not crushed; perplexed, but not in despair; 9 persecuted, but not abandoned; struck down, but not destroyed. 10 We always carry around in our body the death of Jesus, so that the life of Jesus may also be revealed in our body." Listen to what our brother, Paul is telling us in these verses. We are the jars of clay, the vessels that God wants to use to share the treasure. The "treasure" is the good news of Christ. Paul goes on to say that we are hard-pressed but not crushed; perplexed, but not in despair; persecuted, but not abandoned; struck down, but not destroyed. This means that we may be down, but we are never out! It is God's awesome favor that sees us through these trials. And why? The scripture tells us that the "all-surpassing power is from God!"

The Favor Factor

God is the one who will get us through and He is the one who deserves the glory! When we face terrible trials, ones that seem as if they will do us in, God's unmerited favor shows up to bring us through. When His favor shows up, there is no doubt where it has come from. Because we lack the all-knowing knowledge of God, we need to hear and see examples of His goodness in the lives of others. This knowledge of God's goodness is shared in each and every testimony.

Your story is as important, to the Kingdom of God, as mine. God wants to use our stories so that the good news of Christ continues to spread. Your story sets an expectation for someone who may be going through a similar situation. If God can bring you through that situation, then He can surely do the same for someone else. Don't hold on to your story because of shame or shyness. Go out and tell others about the goodness of Christ. We are all connected in the body of Christ and saved by the same blood.

Faith in Action

What story has God trusted you to tell? It is time you realize that your story will bring glory to the Kingdom. God specifically chose you to face your trials so that you know and others can see His favor upon your life. Share with others so that they too may be aware of the possibilities in their own lives.

Daily Declaration

I will tell someone my story, today. There is someone needs to hear it.

Outro
Congratulations!

Congratulations ... Isn't it a great thing to be one of His favorites? Hopefully, this has been an enjoyable journey and you know, without a doubt that as God's very own, you are His favored. As heirs to royalty, we are chosen to achieve things that we don't deserve, aren't qualified to receive and sometimes not even looking for. That's God's favor, and it far exceeds anything we could ever do on our own.

The Bible says that we are shielded by favor. When we are shielded by something, it means that it completely consumes us so that we are not destroyed by whatever is attacking us. Think of a parent shielding a child during an earthquake or tornado. I envision a parent completely covering the child with their body. Nothing on the child is exposed because they are shielded from head to toe; therefore, nothing can harm the child no matter the direction of the attack. God's favor shields us the same way. We are completely consumed by His favor.

So now that we understand God's favor and its benefits, each of us has a story to tell. It is our declaration of the goodness of God in our lives. Our stories serve as evidence that we have witnessed the glorious favor of God. When we have gone through something we have an obligation to share our story so that those who are wavering will know that there is hope; no matter the situation, if we hold fast to God, then His favor will bring us through.

Faith in Action

Take a moment and reflect, what was your favorite devotion and why? Did you have a favorite declaration that inspired you? What about your story, did you share it with anyone? Now that you know that favor is a lifestyle for a lifetime, go out and share your story.

ABOUT THE AUTHOR

Shaw is an AUTHOR, MOTIVATIONAL SPEAKER, and has worked as a highly accomplished and celebrated EMPOWERMENT SPECIALIST for over 20 years. Few speakers today scan match the unbridled energy and creative passion that she brings when addressing an audience.

Shaw truly has a heart for people and believes that she is walking in her calling to empower and motivate. Her positive, life-affirming attitude is not only the focal point of recently published book, the Favor Factor, it's also at the heart of everything she does.

As an author, Faye has been featured in widely known publications including Rolling Out, based in Atlanta, GA. Shaw's ultimate goal is to help individuals face challenges through the Favor Factor. This book is a dedication and self-help book for both men and women seeking to turn their stress into their success story. This book features devotions and personal life lessons in love, career, finances, wellness, and more.

To find out more information about Faye Shaw, please visit all of the social media outlets as well as website where you can purchase her book. This book is also available where all digital books are sold (Amazon, Barnes and Noble, etc.). She is currently available as an expert speaker for siminars, conferences, and expos.

Please contact PRTeam@epimediagroup.com for more information.